"You knew Shah Jahan,
life and youth, wealth and glory,
they all drift away in the current of time.
You strove, therefore, to perpetuate
only the sorrow of your heart…
Let the splendour of diamond, pearl and ruby
vanish like the magic shimmer of the rainbow.
Only let this one teardrop, this Taj Mahal,
glisten spotlessly bright on the cheek of time,
forever and ever."

- RABINDRANATH TAGORE

Spirit of the Taj, Mumtaz Mahal…   *…and its author, Emperor Shah Jahan.*

Romancing an era

TAJ

AND BEYOND

In the central octagonal hall of the tomb
on the cenotaphs of Mumtaz Mahal and Shah Jahan
and the marble lattice screen that surrounds them,
the artists reached the zenith of creativity.

First Published by : Brijbasi Art Press Ltd. 2001
Reprint 2005
Text © Brijbasi Art Press Ltd.
Photographs: Gopi Gajwani and D.N. Dube

ISBN 81-87902-00-0

Processed, printed and bound at
Brijbasi Art Press Ltd.
New Delhi, India

Romancing an era

TAJ
AND BEYOND

Photographs by Gopi Gajwani
and D. N. Dube
Text by Anupma Chandwani

BRIJBASI

THE TAJ

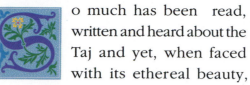

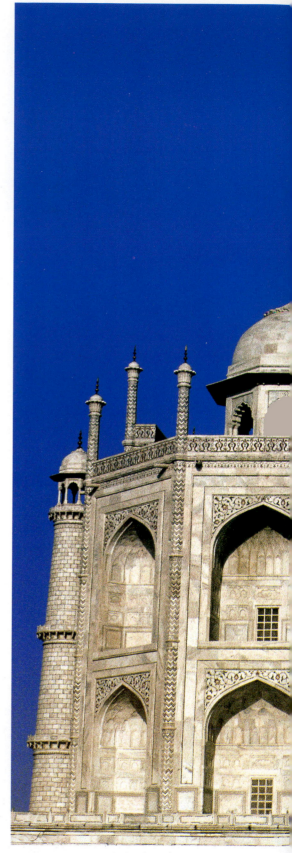

So much has been read, written and heard about the Taj and yet, when faced with its ethereal beauty, you never cease to wonder could the hands of mortals create such an eternal signature of love! If a dream could find an expression, it would surely be the Taj Mahal. With its stunningly perfect contours, it seems to be frozen in time; a love basking in the glory and splendour of an era that stands unparalleled for eternity.

Young prince Khurram was a handsome lad of fifteen when he first lay eyes on Arjumand Banu selling beads and silks at the Meena Bazaar. He went up to her stall and for want of an excuse to communicate, asked the price of the first object he could lay his hands on. "How much is this glass piece worth?" asked the prince. "This is no piece of glass but a rare diamond. You cannot afford it, it's ten thousand rupees!" she exclaimed. Khurram took out the money, gave it to her and left with an impression that was to stay on his mind till the day he died. On returning this 'lofty son of fortune,' as Jahangir calls him in his memoirs, requested his father seeking the hand of Arjumand Banu in marriage. Jahangir, as if reminded of his own days, immediately consented. But it would be five years before the prince could see her again and astrologers proclaimed the year 1607 auspicious for them to get married. Shah Jahan called her Mumtaz Mahal, the 'chosen one of the palace'.

She was the daughter of Asaf Ali

The monumental vastness of the grand mausoleum stands shimmering to the exclusion of everything around.

Khan, Nur Jahan's brother and prime minister of Shah Jahan; grand daughter of the respected Itmad-ud-daulah. Mumtaz Mahal was sensitive, artistic and as well read as her aunt but unlike her was more compassionate, more humane and what of her loveliness! With aristocratic features, her heavenly beauty was perfect; the moon, said the court poets, hid its face in shame.

She never left his side and accompanied him even when he went to fight wars. She bore fourteen children in their nineteen years of marriage, seven of whom died in infancy. When she was expecting her fourteenth child, she accompanied Shah Jahan as he set out to the heart of Deccan for Burhanpur to subdue the forces of Khan Jahan Lodhi. The Emperor was reluctant as the journey was long but she was adamant and wanted to accompany him as she had done always.

In June 1631 news of the birth of a girl child reached Shah Jahan even as the battle was on. Next day at dawn he was summoned by his favourite daughter Jahanara – all was not well with his wife. The Emperor rushed to her and was told that the queen had heard the child crying in her womb; it was a bad omen and foretold death. As the Emperor knelt beside her bed, she whispered her last three wishes – take care of our children, never marry again and build a monument of our love for the world to remember! Soon after she died.

Shah Jahan was inconsolable. For a week he did not eat, drink or allow anybody inside the room he had locked himself in. On the eighth day when he

The outward tilt of the minars ensures that should they fall, the dome would still be safe.

came out his face had aged with grief, his back bent and his hair had all turned white. He ordered a two-year mourning for the entire kingdom. For the next twenty two years, the shattered Emperor had only one obsession - to build a monument for her, the likes of which humanity would never had imagined or could ever think of creating again. And so he did! An Emperor's obsession with his grief finally resulted in a wonder being created.

The task of building the mausoleum tested all that the human mind and body was capable of. For a better visual ambience, the river Yamuna is said to have been diverted from its original course to the foot of the Taj. The entire area was dug up and filled with sediment to prevent seepage. Foundation was laid with stone-in-lime masonry, in below water level areas and with brick-in-lime in above water areas. A series of deep wells with rubble-in-lime inside and stone masonry outside were built along the riverside to counteract the force of the river. Teams of oxen and buffaloes were used to cart huge blocks of marble from Rajasthan. The technical and scientific skill of the times is evident from the techniques used to lay a strong foundation, to raise the grand dome and evenly distribute its weight. The height of the platform was sufficiently raised to avoid all possible threats from floods.

Taj Mahal literally, 'Crown of Palaces', is clearly the result of indulgence that comes from an overflowing treasury and political security. On Shah Jahan's death when his son Aurangzeb asked his father's wealth to be evaluated, he was told that it would take an expert no less than fourteen years to

assess. At least…an infinite number of corals, topaz and other precious stones, 750 pounds of pearls, 1000 gold-studded saddles with jewels, 50,000 pounds of gold plate, wrought gold and silver, 275 pounds of emeralds, countless uncut diamonds, necklaces, Chinese and porcelain vessels…at Agra, a similar treasury in Delhi and three times as much in Lahore. Only Shah Jahan could have done it. No wonder then that the great poet of our times Sahir Ludhyanvi said that the Taj was a joke an Emperor chose to play on his poor subjects.

The Taj is a garden tomb laid in a slight deviation from the Mughal Char Bagh style, in a rectangular shape complex aligned north-south. At the southern end, an immense gateway 46 metre wide and 30.5 metre high stands impressively as if guarding a precious jewel within. This gate is approached through a series of arcaded galleries that once served as markets and rest rooms. Three smaller gateways guard entry to this red sandstone structure. A rectangular frame of calligraphic decoration borders the grand arched fascade and cupolas in white marble render it a royalty dignity. An inscription reads, 'So

enter as one of his servants; and enter into His garden.' At the corners rise octagonal towers topped with domes in white marble. The arch of this gateway contains the Taj perfectly within itself and presents to the beholder a jewel it has treasured through centuries. The complex is so beautifully united that it gives due prominence to the Taj; yet this unity does not obscure the individuality of each of these elements.

Unlike most monuments that lie at the centre of the Char Bagh layout, the tomb is placed at the northern end, with an expanse of lush green carpet between the tomb and the gateway. A long stretch of water channel with fountains, with rows of cypress trees on either side, reflects the Taj like Narcissus looking at his own reflection. Two identical buildings in red sandstone with marble domes stand on either side, a mosque on the west and a building referred to as *jawab* (answer) on the east. Thus named, its only purpose seems to be to provide a balance to the mosque on the west. Some also call it *mehmankhana* or guest quarters and say that it was used by the royal guests. A huge archway dominates both these

Verses from Quran *adorn the façades of the Taj. Right: Huge arches with marble lattice screens characterise the gleaming Taj walls.*

structures. Exquisite floral patterns adorn the ceiling. On the walls and the floor are geometric patterns in sandstone interspersed with white marble. On the face of it, marble and red sand stone seem to be the primary ingredients; on the contrary, they form only an outer clothing for *lakhauri inth* (thin, square bricks) and lime mortar that have been used for the entire construction.

The balance of all these structures, gardens and waterways is such that rather than interfere with the existence of the tomb, they define the space it rises from. Majestic and sensuous, it reflects the spirit embodied within. The moods of the Taj vary from dawn when its soft milky whiteness as if descends from heaven and in a searing mid-day heat it glistens like a jewel, to "the enchanting tint of a pale and lovely rose" and tired by night sleeps "among the stars like a great pearl." By moonlight "its seduction is irresistible."

Strangely, the architect of this eighth wonder of the world remains unknown, though several sources mention the name of a Turk, Ustad Isa Efandi. During his reign, Shah Jahan had patronised the finest of craftsmen and engineers from all over the world. Even to a layman, who has no clue of design, of architecture, of style, the first observation staring like a blatant fact, is the perfect symmetry of the monument; the only asymmetrical aspect of the monument being the cenotaph of the man who conceived its very idea. The mausoleum is marked by a bulbous dome that stands over a square base, sur-

The archways are bordered with verses from the Quran *while the spandrels reveal arabesque ornamentation.*

16

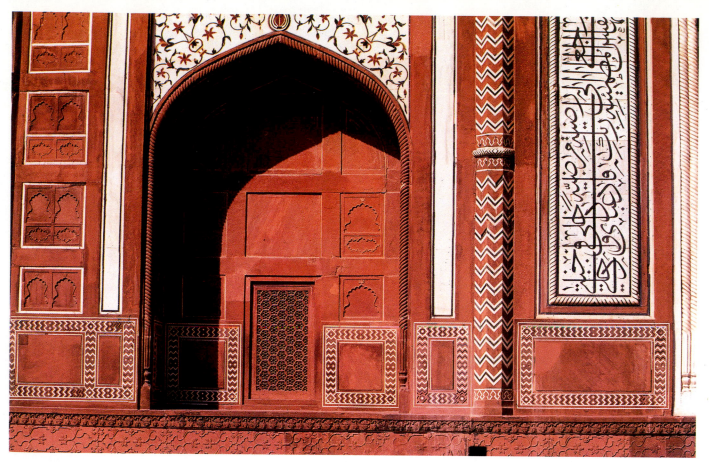

Preceding page: Every single alphabet from 19 chapters of the Quran *has been cut and inlaid with precision. The entire* Quran *was consciously avoided; should the structure ever topple, there would be no disrespect to the Holy Book.*
Above: Two red sandstone buildings flanking either side of the tomb have been embellished in a similar manner as the Taj itself.
Right: The central water channel reflects the Taj like Narscissus looking at his own reflection.

rounded by four slender towers "like a beautiful princess, surrounded by four ladies-in-waiting." What thoughtfulness that these *minars*(towers) tilt a little to the outside - should these break, no damage would be caused to the tomb, as their outward lean would ensure a fall away from the tomb.

As you move from the southern gate towards the Taj, its monumental vastness slowly unfurls and it stands shimmering to the exclusion of everything around. From the centre of a 5.79 metre high marble plinth rises a majestic tomb to a height of 74.2 metres. An immense arch that dominates the façade is framed with inscriptions from the *Quran*, with spandrels revealing arabesque ornamentation. Multiple alcoves, both inside and outside break the monotony of the façade. Verses from 19 of 30 chapters of the *Quran* are inscribed all over the

Taj complex. Calligraphic genius is displayed in creation of such a perspective that as you go on reading upwards, the words appear to be of the same size all along the vertical path that goes as high as a contemporary twelve-tiered building. Interestingly, of the 20,000 men who worked for twenty two years towards making a reality of an Emperor's dream, the only signatures thought worthy of display were those of the calligrapher - "written by the insignificant being Amanat Khan Shirazi," it says at the base of the interior dome.

The onion-shaped bulbous double-dome of the Taj Mahal is an architectural and an engineering feat. The outer dome rising to a height of 44.4 metres from the base to the apex of the finial defines the skyline, while the inner dome, 24.35 metres high, balances the height of the inner central hall. The

space between the inner and the outer dome is almost the size of this hall. Ismail Afandi from Turkey, who had also worked for the Ottomans, is said to have designed this magnificence and to cast the gold crown was Qazim Khan from Lahore.

Balancing the height of the dome are four *chatris* (cupolas) rising from the corners of the dome base. By the time the Taj was created, the distinctions that marked the typical styles of Hindu and Islamic architecture had disappeared - they blended so well into each other that it was difficult to tell them apart. No wonder then that these *chatris* so typically Hindu in their concept naturally seem to blend with the dome they surround. Shah Jahan had learnt a lot from his grandfather Akbar. Being a part of a process of cultural

synthesis, in fact, having affected it in a lot of ways, it was unlikely that he would not have contributed to the architecture and design of the monument closest to his heart.

The dazzling white marble from Makrana in Rajasthan has been handled with such care that just the right balance of ornamentation has enhanced its own beauty. Elegant lilies and tulips frame the dado panels containing

Chatris, *typically Hindu in their concept, were an integral part of Mughal architecture.*

white marble Iris - the flower of death. Such panels adorn the lower part of the walls all over the mausoleum. But what is probably breath taking is the perfection of a style called *pietra dura*, the inlay work on marble. At places blooms have been composed using as many as 64 pieces of cornelian. The days when the Taj stood in its complete grandeur, the white marble was embellished with diamonds from Golconda, quartz from the Himalayas, turquoise from Tibet, cornelian from Baghdad, jade and crystal from China, coral from the Red Sea, lapis lazuli from Sri Lanka, malachite from Russia, in all, 43 varieties of precious and semi-precious stones from around the world – half-inch inlaid in the wonder stone from Makrana. So perfect is the inlay that a needlepoint passed over the marble finds no obstructions. Even the verses from *Quran* have each dot and each alphabet cut and inlaid with precision. The Mughal love for gardens is clearly reflected through the flowers created using the *pietra dura* style, the most common being lilies and honeysuckles. It is said that one bloom on the tomb of Mumtaz Mahal was inlaid with 35 different precious stones.

Eight rooms connected by a corridor running through them, surround the silent octagonal central hall. Translucent glass that separates this hall and the rooms outside, allows dim light to penetrate through, just enough to create an aura of serenity. And it is here on the cenotaphs and the eight feet high octagonal screen surrounding them, that

the artisans, designers, inlay artists have created worlds of wonder. Even if the artisans wanted to they would never be able to repeat the Taj, for, it is said, that the Emperor had their hands chopped off. So perfectly delicate is the workmanship, it seems a mere touch could ruin it.

Like all tombs that distinguish those of men and women, the cenotaph of Shah Jahan has an inkwell over it and that of Mumtaz Mahal a slate, implying that a man writes his desires on a woman's heart. *Markad munavar Arjumand Banu Begum mukhatib Mumtaz Mahal 1040* - 'Tomb of the beautiful Arjumand Banu Begum named Mumtaz Mahal who died in 1040 Hijri,' it says on her cenotaph and the epitaph on that of Shah Jahan reads, 'The sacred sepulchre of His Most Exalted Majesty, Dweller of Paradise, the Second Lord of Constellation, the king Shah Jahan, may his mausoleum ever flourish, 1706.' The cenotaph of Mumtaz Mahal has verses from the *Quran* one of which reads, 'Fear ye not! Neither be ye grieved! But rejoice ye in the paradise which ye have been promised.' With a pearl canopy hanging over the grave of Mumtaz Mahal, a gold railing encrusted with precious stones originally enclosed the cenotaphs. But for fear of vandalism, Shah Jahan had these replaced with the marble lattice screens that stand as "a triumph of oriental decorative art."

Below these cenotaphs lie the actual tombs in a serene basement chamber. Ninety-nine names of Allah have been inscribed on the tomb of Mumtaz Mahal. It is said that bowls and bowls full of jewels were placed on her

24

On top of the southern gate of the Taj
complex, eleven chatris in white marble render
the structure a Royal Dignity.

tomb once and the gates into this tomb were made of silver. Persian carpets lay below and from the ceiling hung exquisite chandeliers.

No single monument has evoked such varied emotions as the Taj. From Rabindra Nath Tagore who thought that the Taj was a tear drop on the face of Eternity, to Sahir Ludhyanvi, who does not think it anything beyond brash indulgence, most remain mesmerised by its feminine grace. "It is Mumtaz herself, radiant in her youthful beauty… a tribute to the grace of Indian womanhood…" Shah Jahan died looking at this "most perfect pearl on an azure ground" from the Agra Fort where he had been imprisoned by his son. And he who had made daily journeys by boat from the Fort to the Taj everyday for all the years that it took to build, he who had come here to pay his respect as if at a holy shrine, thus praises the Taj Mahal in the *Badshah Nama*

…Its walls and gates glitter with gems.
The air is there fresh and delightful
like brilliancy of pearl.
The architect of this sacred edifice
Brought water for it from the
fountain of grace.
On this sacred edifice of high renown
Showers of mercy are ever pouring.
Should guilty seek asylum here,
Like one pardoned,
he becomes free from sin.
Should a sinner make his way to this
mansion,
All his past sins are sure to be washed
away…

A blossoming love that grew to an obsession and ended in *ibadat!*

*Between the southern gateway and the tomb
of the Taj lies a long stretch of water channel with
rows of cypress trees on either side.*

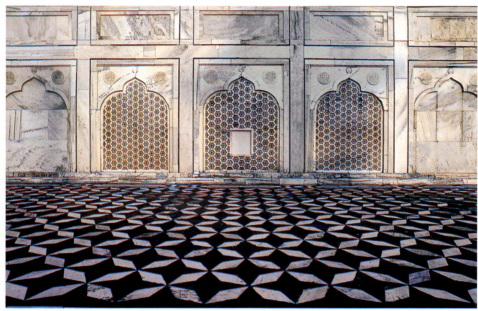

Unlike Itmad-ud-daulah where every inch has been carved or inlaid, at the Taj Mahal just the right ornamentation enhances the beauty of the white marble.
Right: The dome of the Taj placed on a square base is an architectural and engineering feat.

Left: An archway of marble lattice screens leads into the central octagonal hall.
Above: The cenotaph of Mumtaz Mahal visible straight through the arch of the eight feet high octagonal screen surrounding the cenotaphs. On the left is the tomb of Emperor Shah Jahan, the only asymmetrical aspect of the grand mausoleum.
Right: 'Bismillah Al Rehman Al Raheem' is the beginning of anything auspicious in Islam.

The pietra dura *style found perfection on the tombs of Shah Jahan and his beloved queen.*
Right: Below the false tombs in the octagonal hall lie the actual ones in a basement chamber. Like the tombs of all men and women in Islam that of the Emperor has an inkwell over it and that of the queen, a slate.

The delicate workmanship displayed in this central hall is so perfect that a needle-point passed over the inlay finds no obstruction.

In its absolute grandeur, the marble on the Taj was embellished with 43 varieties of precious and semi-precious stones from around the world. At places single blooms have been composed from as many as 64 pieces of cornelian.

38

The River Yamuna that bends around the Taj is said to have been thus diverted for a better visual ambience.
Right: Here on the opposite bank, they say, Shah Jahan had dreamt of a black Taj for himself and the two he would join with a silver bridge. Who knows…for, today there are just open fields.

A Mughal Extravaganza
BEYOND THE TAJ

 he Taj is not the beginning of an architectural genre, rather the culmination of a style that found its seeds at the Humayun's tomb in Delhi and was finally taken to perfection by Jahangir and Shah Jahan. Agra was to be the home that bred such perfection. This city of Taj finds mention in Hindu mythology as Agraban or 'paradise' and first gained prominence when Sikandar Lodhi moved his capital from Delhi to Agra in 1502. Here he built a small fort and around it grew a township called Sikandra, after his name. The battle of Panipat finally sounded the death knell of the Lodhi dynasty and thus lay the foundations of what was to become one of the most splendid and glorious empires that history would witness - the Mughal Empire.

Babur, the first of the Mughals was greatly disappointed by Hindustan. The heat and dust compounded by the lack of planned towns and gardens was not what he had come here for. His great ancestor Timur had gone back to Central Asia for the same reason - Babur decided to stay and **Aram Bagh** is what he gave to Agra. This was the first of the beautiful Mughal Gardens that flowed down four centuries to reach its pinnacle at the Viceroy's Palace - today the Rashtrapati Bhawan in New Delhi. In its heyday, the Aram Bagh with its numerous pools, fountains and pavilions built amidst fruit-bearing trees

Seen from above the Khas Mahal in the Agra Fort, the Taj beckons from beyond the Yamuna.

and floweri
tings of par
nately, wh
today is not

Babur sp
years conso
tory goes, B
his son Hur
self that fina
so in 1530
throne – a w
dling what he
shifted to De
(old fort) as l
rarily forced
Afghan nobl
after regaini
bling down t
widow built a
that was an a
of marble ar
the later Mug

Akbar, t
Hindustan e
deserts of Si
He came to
thirteen and c
empire reach
stretched fr

46

Left: Above the dado level, floral and geometric patterns, wine bottles and fruits, express themselves in typical Persian style.
Top: The paintings on the walls and ceiling that were partly done in gold were subject to vandalism by Suraj Mal Jat. Lord Curzon in 1905 restored whatever little was possible.
Above: Nur Jahan is said to have built this mausoleum for her father Mirza Gias Beg and mother Ismet Begum with her own money, meher *given to her by Jahangir at the time of their wedding.*

Top: The square mausoleum, 70 feet in length is set on a platform with hexagonal towers topped by cupolas, raised on its four corners.
Above: The dado level outside, displays coloured geometric patterns that run around the tomb.
Right page: The delicate carvings adorning the façades feel like 'architecture of Braille'.

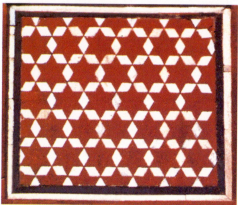

Preceding Page: Akbar's mausoleum is stark, grand and original like the emperor himself.
Above Left: Bold geometric and floral patterns adorn the gateways of the tomb.
Above: Akbar's tomb at Sikandra, is a five-tiered structure, following the Panch Mahal style at Fatehpur Sikri.

A highly ornate entrance, the Sunehri Mahal done in Persian style (left) leads to Akbar's tomb in a basement chamber (above) that is surprisingly simple and bare compared to its exterior. Following Page: Akbar's tomb spreading across 123 acres, provided 44 rooms for the families of subsequent Mughal rulers to be burried here.

Venerating a saint
FATEHPUR SIKRI

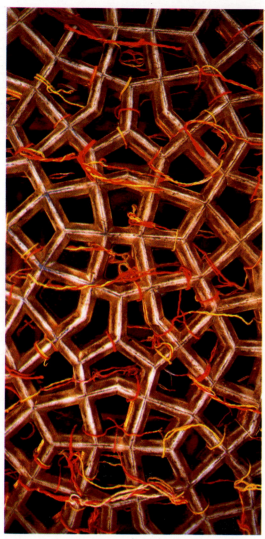

Above: Till today people seek benediction by way of tying red threads on marble screens that surround the shrine of Sheikh Salim Chisti, asking for wishes to be fulfilled.
Opposite page: The marble jallis *on the walls of the* durgah *are carved out of single pieces of marble. Providing a transluscent view to the outside world, they are considered works of exquisite craftsmanship.*

With all his great political insight, keen intellect and religious tolerance, Akbar's cause for concern was the absence of an heir to the Mughal throne. Finally, with the blessings of a Sufi saint Salim Chisti, three sons were born to Akbar. The first, born to Jodha Bai in 1569 he named Salim, after the saint. History handed him down as Jahangir. In commemoration, he built a new capital Fatehpur Sikri, 40 kilometres west of Agra - a shrine in honour of Salim Chisti and his own palaces next to it. Around the shrine he built a mosque that is said to be a smaller version of the one at Mecca. Akbar had this shrine built in red sandstone; later Jahangir replaced this with his favourite stone, the white marble.

Fatehpur Sikri remained Akbar's capital for only 16 years from 1570 to 1586. Referred to as the incomplete city it was deserted as quickly as it was built. Why Akbar moved back to Agra is still unknown; while some say it was because of water shortage, others feel it was too isolated a place to rule from.

The walled city of Fatehpur Sikri does not attract as much as a glorious township that grew so quickly, as for its diverse buildings, their scale and the spaces they define. The fusion of Hindu and Islamic architecture is awe-inspiring. These buildings are less towering and closer to the base, a prominent feature being the *jharokas* or windows inspired from Rajasthani architecture. If there is a single complex that

represents the Emperor in thought, in style, in living, it is the Fatehpur Sikri. Other than the shrine of the saint that stands in white marble, the red sandstone predominates – the remarkable stone, soft like clay, hard enough to be cut and carved and strong enough to last centuries.

The walls of Fatehpur Sikri enclose an area of $16\frac{1}{2}$ sq. miles and once had nine gates. The only gate through which one enters this walled city is the Agra gate. The mosque and the palaces are a mile inside the walls of the fort. Fifty-two steps lead to the Bulland Darwaza, the grand gateway at the southern entrance of the mosque that towers majestically at a height of 134 feet. From the base of the steps it measures 176 feet and is the highest gateway in India celebrating Akbar's victory over Khandesh in 1601. With lotus motifs, geometric designs and verses from the *Quran*, this majestic gateway reflects a remarkable synthesis of divergent cultures. This was the gate used by people to come to the mosque. Akbar used the gate on the east that came to be called the Akbari Darwaza. On either side of this gate are stairs leading to the top for guards to announce the Emperor's arrival.

As you enter, the *durgah*(shrine) of Sheikh Salim Chisti stands humbly in white marble. People flock the *durgah*, seeking benediction and asking whatever they wish for. Huge single piece marbles have been cut in various designs to form *jallis* or marble screens around the shrine. Thousands come month after month, tie red threads on *jallis* and when wishes are fulfilled, come and break the thread. A

magnificent frame of sandalwood covered with mother-of-pearl stands over the grave. Outside, the serpentine brackets that curve upwards from pillars to the ceiling, create an impression of arms being raised in the glory of Allah. The sound of *qawalli* fills the air adding to the holy ambience. The mosque is at its best during the month of *Ramzan*. Eight days ending on *Id-Ul-Fitr*, it comes alive with celebrations, dances and *qawallis* that are sung through the night. Descendents of Sheikh Salim Chisti continue to live in the Sikri village and those deceased are still buried inside this mosque complex.

Eighty-four rooms that were used as school for children surround a huge central courtyard. Even today children from the village come and learn here. The mosque is on the west and prayers are held 5 times a day like in any other mosque. What is visibly different is that the pillars on one side of the prayer room reflect Islamic architecture and on the other side have Hindu motifs. The splendidly ornamented sanctum has a central dome with floral designs and on the wall verses from the Quran have been calligraphed in gold. Built on the highest point of the ridge, the mosque complex can accommodate as many as 10,000 worshippers.

North East of the mosque, Akbar built his own palaces that are a visual treat even today. The intermingling of various styles of architecture blending all religions is reflected through sheer poetry in red sandstone that stands witness to an era, history can find no parallel to. Typical to the Mughal palaces are small doorways. This enforced bowing in respect before entering the

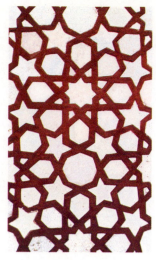

Above: Geometric patterns typical of Islamic architecture are found throughout the mosque that stands to the left of the Chisti shrine.
Right: Inside the mosque stands a small white pedestal for the priest. On its right is seen a small arch called mehrab. All mehrabs symbolically open towards Mecca and have been carved along the western wall of the mosque. Devotees face these while in prayer.

palaces. Maharaja Ranjit Singh, one of the greatest Sikh nobles was the only one who put his feet in first, refusing to bow to the mightiest of Mughals. The first of Fatehpur Sikri's palaces is the high-walled Jodha Bai's Palace for Akbar's Hindu queen. Designed like a Rajasthani *haveli*, the blue rooftops done in Chinese plaster still carry the freshness of yesteryears. Akbar built for his Christian wife Mariam the Sunehra Makan or the golden house - once covered with gold, today it looks quite insignificant. Sultana Begum's palace once shone in diamonds and till today is the most impressive with every inch elegantly sculptured into exquisite floral and geometric patterns.

Aкbar's own bedroom, Khwabgah that once had rose water flowing through it, is at the southern end of the complex. On the groundfloor was a huge library of an Emperor who was himself an illiterate – the only philosopher without formal education! In front of his palace is the Anup Talao, a waterbody with four bridges leading to a central platform then used by the *sangeet samrat* (king of music) Tansen.

The whimsical looking Panch Mahal or the Five-tiered Palace was used by the ladies of the court. The sides were covered by *jallis* or carved screens to conceal the royal women from public view when they watched functions from this palace. The five tiers represent the five elements that constitute all life form – its architecture inspired from the Buddhist concept of Pagodas. The lowest floor has 56 beautifully carved columns, no two of which are alike. On the western end is the Birbal Bhawan, a palace for Birbal, one of the most treasured jewels of Akbar's court. With its richly carved Hindu motifs, it is among Fatehpur Sikri's best palaces.

The Diwan-e-Khas (Hall of Private Audience) is a simple looking building outside with rather interesting interiors that may have found inspiration in the Hindu mythology. A stone column rising from the centre of the room blooms into the shape of a flower with carved brackets that unfold upwards from the pillar. The flower holds in it a flat throne that once seated Akbar. Four galleries connect the throne to the corners of the room. The nine doors around the room were for the nine jewels of his court. Seated on this throne, Akbar may well have played *Brahma* incarnate rising from *Vishnu's* lotus.

Above: The palaces of Fatehpur Sikri are endless canvases where the workmanship of artisans glowed under the patronage of Akbar. Right: Verses from Quran *in the sanctum of the mosque still glisten with the freshness of gold.*

Next to the Diwan-e-Khas is Ankh-Michauli, a palace where the Emperor is said to have played hide and seek with the ladies of the harem. They say he always used to play the seeker. This palace was also used to keep official records and served as a treasury. The recesses along the sides had sliding stone slabs where gold and silver coins may have been stored. Just outside this palace is a canopied structure that was probably the astrologer's seat.

On the north-east end is the Diwan-e-Am (Hall of Public Audience) that has a central courtyard. A round hook in the middle of this courtyard had in those days an elephant tied to it, Akbar's favourite elephant whose grave is on the northern end beyond the palaces. He would carry out the task of crushing the guilty to death. Beside this hall is a game-board blocked out on the floor that was used to play the game of *pachisi* or *chauser* where slave girls were used as pieces.

It was here at Fatehpur Sikri that Akbar founded his new religion - Din-e-Ilahi. The religion died with the king as did this capital and a once living, glorious centre of a grand empire today stands abandoned. But its essence till today is embodied in the mosque, at the shrine and in the palaces that were home to creators of such epochal events in time!

The Mughals
(From Babur to Shah Jahan)

Emperor	Title	Birth-Death	Ruled	
Zahir-ud-din	Babur (The Tiger)	1483-1530	1526-1530	
Nasir-ud-din	Humayun (Loyal)	1508-1556	1530-1556	*(Ousted by Sher Shah Sur for 15 years during this period)*
Jallal-ud-din	Akbar (The Great)	1542-1605	1556-1605	
Nur-ud-din	Jahangir (World Conqueror)	1569-1627	1605-1627	
Shahab-ud-din	Shah Jahan (Emperor of the world)	1592-1666	1627-1658	

On either side of the Bulland Darwaza (right), grand gateway leading to the Fatehpur Sikri mosque, stand huge wooden doors with shoe-horses (left) that have been nailed by people asking for the well being of their animals.
Above: At the centre of the mosque complex at Fatehpur Sikri, the shrine of Sheikh Salim Chisti glows in white marble.

Left: The first visible structure on entering the Bulland Darwaza is the serene looking durgah of Sheikh Salim Chisti. Above: A magnificent sandle-wood frame ornamented with mother-of-pearl stands over the actual grave of the saint.

The Diwan-e-Khas at Fatehpur Sikri is one of its most intriguing buildings. From the centre of the room rises a pillar ending in beautifully carved brackets to hold a flat throne for the Emperor. Small galleries connect the throne to the corners of the room.

Left: Anoop Talao at Fatehpur Sikri, seated the sangeet samrat, Tansen. On the left, two top storeys of the Panch Mahal soar above the other structures.

Above: The Panch Mahal with its five storeys follows the Buddhist concept of Pagodas with each of its successive tiers shorter than the preceding one.

Right: Alcoves have been carved inside many of the palaces. They served various purposes from holding candles, to being used as shelves, jewelry and treasure boxes.

Photo credits

Gopi Gajwani

Cover, Pgs. 2-3, 8-9, 10-11, 12-13, 14-15, 16-17, 18-19, 20, 21, 22-23, 26-27, 30, 33 (top), 40-41, 44 (left), 46, 47, 48, 49, 50, 51, 52, 53, 54-55, 56-57, 58-59, 60, 61, 62, 63, 64-65, 66-67, 68, 69, 70, 71 (below), 72-73, 74-75, 76-77, 79 (right), 82, 83, 84, 85, 86, 87, 88 (below), 89, 91, 92(left), 94, 95, 96.

D.N. Dube

Pgs. 1, 4-5, 6-7, 24-25, 28-29, 31, 32, 33 (below), 34-35, 36-37, 38, 39, 44 (right), 71 (top), 78, 80-81, 88(top), 90, 92 (right), Backcover.

Brijbasi

Pgs. 42-43.